Human
Resources in
Crisis

Human Resources in
Crisis

RUDOLF HARTONG

authorHOUSE®

AuthorHouse™
1663 Liberty Drive
Bloomington, IN 47403
www.authorhouse.com
Phone: 1-800-839-8640

Published by AuthorHouse   01/25/2013

ISBN: 978-1-4817-8260-9 (sc)
ISBN: 978-1-4817-8283-8 (e)

This book is printed on acid-free paper.

This booklet is based on my experiences and observations of forty years working in human resources and management positions.

Rudolf Hartong

For Johanna

For her help, her support in writing this booklet,
and for forty years of marriage

Preface

This small book about 'human resources in crisis' is based on my forty years of working experience in human resources (HR) and general management. It is neither a scientific book nor an academic study based on theories, but it is a book based on a very practical approach. I will focus on human resources because I see that it is in crisis. It has lost its professionalism as well as the respect and the trust of employees. In general it has lost its identity. In this book I will explain how I have experienced this and my worry about its lack of contribution to the success of a company in the form that HR now takes. I will give examples, but I will also provide suggestions to revive human resources.

I am writing this book because of the above-described development in human resources, what I called 'the crisis in HR'. I have reason to do that because HR can really make a difference as one of the main contributors to the success of a company and its employees, which I have proven and shown in my career. It is also based on my professional education in human resources (in HR at Sociale Akademie for four years and a *Voortgezette Opleiding* (continuing education) also in HR for two years in The Netherlands). The forty years of work have been a journey together with my family, living in seven countries (Spain, Switzerland, Denmark, Sweden, The Netherlands, Russia and Indonesia), where we experienced different cultures, languages, challenges, and historical changes. During this time I worked for twenty-two years in human resources positions and for eighteen years in general management. Based on my experiences this book is intended for everyone in any country.

The book is divided into two sections. Section 1 is concerned with describing and identifying the problem: the crisis. It starts with the historical evolution of HR during the last fifty years and goes on to look at developments that hurt the professionalism of HR as well as providing actual observations with examples. Section 2 is concerned with a possible solution to the crisis; it looks at an approach that would enable HR to regain trust and respect, not ignoring new developments and the role of the managing director (MD)/general manager (GM). This section ends with a positive recognition of human resources in a company. Both sections together provide a complete overview of developments in HR, for readers to think about similar developments in their own companies.

Human resources and general management are linked, but each role will be clarified in this book. Both positions are important because you cannot improve HR without understanding how a managing director (MD) can help. HR, as I see it, is part of the responsibility of a managing director or general manager of a company. The MD, assisted by HR, is responsible for forming and executing an HR policy in a company. In multinational companies, the global HR policy is developed by top management, and local management in a particular country of course has to follow the guidelines of the global company in order to strengthen the company culture. What I emphasize in my book is that more attention has to be given to the local situation of a local company and its unique culture. By focusing on that unique cultural element, not by ignoring it, you can find creative solutions for local situations, which can contribute a lot to the success of the company. This book is written for staff in both MD/GM and HR positions so that both may work together to improve HR and its revival.

I hope that by understanding the challenges and value that HR brings to an organization we can begin to implement changes and improve the lives of everyone.

Rudolf Hartong
December 2012

Acknowledgements

I would like to thank very much Ilias Aliev, Ton Coenen, Rose and Henry Gan, and our children, Suzanne, Maarten, Frank, Irene, and Paul, and their partners, for their very valuable contributions, comments, and reactions that have made this booklet what it is now.

The pictures were taken by Maarten Hartong.

CONTENTS

Section 1

Identifying the problem: the crisis in human resources

Section 2

How HR can regain trust and respect and fulfil the right role in a company management team

SECTION 1

IDENTIFYING THE PROBLEM:
THE CRISIS IN HUMAN RESOURCES

A. Human resources' DEVELOPMENT

Introduction

It is always important to take a historical perspective on the development of a profession, in this case that of human resources (HR). I will describe how the 'old' personnel department evolved into HR from the 1960s to the 21st century as well as the changes in the different roles HR has played until today.

When I started my study and professional life in HR, it was the time of growth, 'flower power', freedom, and actions for more democracy in society, universities, and colleges. The established power in universities and academies was (temporarily) overthrown by student councils. Exams were not necessary any more, and students should evaluate one another. 'Power to the suppressed' was an often-used expression.

Business and companies were, in general, doing well; growth and welfare (like state pensions and social security) were new experiences. The study of Sociology became a fashion. Everybody was 'socially' interested. Business and making money were 'dirty'. Political parties on the 'left' were dominating the political landscape. There was enthusiasm in the air—a kind of 'social revolution'.

When I finished my study and started my first job, I was immediately confronted with a reality shock in my new business environment; the 'social revolution' had not taken place in business/companies/factories.

I assume that a lot of my student colleagues as well as psychologists and sociologists at that time must have been frustrated with this reality. However, most of them were not, as they were working in governmental institutes and organizations where this social revolution was popular and where good salaries were paid (better than in commercial business at that time).

So my step into 'real' business was not so common. 'Democratic management' was not heard of, was not common, and was not accepted in business, and it still isn't today. It was not very realistic because the decision-making process would take too long while you have to act quickly in changing situations like markets, competition, and products.

1. The 1960s and 1970s: the administrator

Personnel, as the HR department was called at that time, was executing what I call the ABC of HR: recruiting, selection, introduction, and training. It was often headed or managed by an ex-military officer, an ex-production manager, or by the financial manager. They were heads of personnel, loyal to top management. As the profession of

HR was not fully developed at this time, they were selected on the basis of their loyalty. Sometimes they were over-complete managers, for whom management had to find a job. For instance, a factory manager, who was not in his right place in production, was offered the personnel job. They acted like an administrator. The position did not carry high status, and normally this (male) person was the lowest paid in the management team. You saw some improvement as companies recruited professionally educated HR staff in starting positions—like me. But most of the top HR positions were filled by top management selecting loyal, non-HR educated persons.

'Administrators', as I called them, were serious, often capable, and good-willing people, who tried to execute what the CEO (chief executive officer) or MD was telling them. In the management team they had often the lowest status, next to the communication/information manager.

In short the administrator (female administrators were not present) was a good soldier who executed what was decided by top management. An example: A request for a salary increase was handled by the 'administrators' as if they had to pay it from their own pocket.

It was quite an experience when I started my first job working for a head of personnel and a big contrast with the 'social revolution' of my student time, where equal rights, labour rights, personal development, and democratic companies were hot topics. But I learned a lot, especially the ABC of personnel, the basic tools at that time, which were well developed, often with the help of outside consultant companies.

2. The 1970s and 1980s: the professional

Because of the developments in society (professionalism in many directions), the HR function started to develop. It expanded and developed by recruiting, for instance, specialists in employee relations and employee contracts (lawyers). Even big companies employed social workers. Also management development programs started in big companies, such as career development programs. The employment of trainees became a topic, as well as future leadership programs and so forth. A lot of activities took place, and HR became pro-active in the organizations.

Strikes and social unrest were factors that companies tried to avoid. Labour contracts were negotiated. An annual social report was a new item, in which companies tried to explain their position and policies towards their employees. 'Co-workers' was a new fashionable name for employees in this period. There was attention for the individual employee, even for special cases (disabled people were sporadically employed, in spite of some laws). In this period the name changed from personnel to human resources.

HR departments were growing, and with their specialties and professionalism HR became a clearly recognized department/ function in an organization. It got a better name and profile.

HR had a function to advise management on social issues (employee issues/human capital) in the company and also on social development outside the company. Contact with labour unions was often delegated and managed by HR professionals, no longer being the responsibility of the MD or GM of a company.

That growth in status and power made it a more important and an 'independent' function in the management team. The salaries of the top managers in HR improved, and although they were not often in the executive team of a company (sales/marketing, finance, engineering/production), HR was not the lowest in ranking any more. That became communications/information and a new department: environment.

3. The 1990s: the multitasker

As the development of HR continued it became a kind of 'octopus'. Their influence stretched from recruitment/selection to the end of a person's career, like arranging pension training courses for employees who would soon retire. The whole life of a working employee was under control. Attention was paid to all aspects of an employee's working life. From a very positive influence with an innovative approach twenty years ago, it became a bureaucratic department, and its costs—to run all of these functions and activities—in turn went up. One way to bring costs down was the introduction of outsourcing tasks like making use of specialized recruitment companies. During the economic crisis, which started towards the end of the twentieth century, attention and critique was on HR with their big organizations and costs.

Besides being very busy and working as a multitasker, the HR function did not develop very much. (It was too busy.) In my opinion, it was, from a professional point of view, a time of 'stand still'. HR had what it wanted: power and influence. It became a 'business partner' in the management team—something that many HR directors had wanted for many years. Previously they had too often been seen as representing the 'soft' part of the business.

Well-known universities, organizations, and institutes were asking for change and for attention to be paid to new trends like, for instance, a need for real leadership—as compared to 'management'. It became fashionable to use these new terminologies; top managers suddenly became 'leaders'. The name 'leader' was absorbed more as a fashionable term rather than as an action for real change. This happened with many more 'fashionable' name inventions.

In the 1960s and 1970s quality circles were very popular (a concept that was developed in Japan in 1962 by Kaoru Ishikawa). A 'quality circle' is a volunteer group of employees from the same work area who meet together to discuss workplace improvement. The aim was continuous quality improvements at the shop floor level. At the end of the twentieth century the idea no longer functioned. Management development as a management tool was popular, but it was not functioning; it was not well implemented or well followed by central HR, and it was not supported by top management.

New, from the United States, came the balanced scorecard (BSC), a new management tool described by Dr R. Kaplan and D. Norton. For many years, according to my opinion, everything worked well without a BSC, but, for some reason, it was introduced. Probably it was done to additionally compensate a certain level of managers and employees for their work while others got share option plans or other incentives. In that period high-potential employees left because of better and much higher incentives offered elsewhere. Share option plans became popular in this period.

The BSC was widely adapted in the 1990s in Western countries as a performance management tool. It was used by managers to keep track of the execution of activities by the staff within their control and to monitor the consequences (the financial rewards) arising from these actions. It was centrally introduced, and it was cascaded down the organization. This tool was based on four perspectives (financial, customer, business process, and learning and growth) and could contain six to twelve measurements, which were decided by top management. All of these objectives were split into smaller sub-objectives for companies and/or departments within the organization. The whole idea was to get a centrally controlled focus by managers and all staff on the most important items that top management wanted to execute. 'You get what you measure' was the slogan. For the employees participating, all was related to a financial incentive or bonus, dependent on the score at the end of the year.

HR was on the sideline during these new introductions, and for a short while these BSC introductions were successful. After a few years of working with this BSC system it became, in my opinion, a faulty instrument. For individuals the money became God, and the attention for the whole company became less important. Employees and managers became focused only on the measurements mentioned in their BSC, as it could influence their score and pay. The total company became less important, and consequently the company culture suffered.

HR became a 'follower', in spite of its power and influence. The first sign of a new revolution (Information Communications/Information

Technology) was already infiltrating into companies, but at the time it went mostly unnoticed.

4. The 21st century: the administrator

A new revolution took place, with a lot of social implications—an IT revolution. This revolution has not only dramatically influenced our daily life but also how we work, communicate, and develop business, including HR.

Computers, iPhones, iPads, and social media channels like Facebook, LinkedIn, and Twitter influenced the ways in which we communicated.

As one of my Russian friends explained to me:

'People become more independent and can use information providers as much as they want. Management becomes less important as information provider. They have their own sources of information. People are much freer in their thinking and have broader views. They have all kinds of information available on the net. They become much less self-sufficient, as they depend much more on the net as the tool. As a consequence they have much less capability to handle all sorts of situations on their own. All these developments combined inevitably lead to people becoming much colder in interpersonal relationships. They do not depend on relationships to get information to get things done, or at least they have the illusion that they don't. It makes people much more cynical. It is much more difficult for companies to maintain a positive motivation of their employees.'

This development also influenced HR. They did not come up with an answer to this development. On the contrary, they started using the IT systems in HR even more! In principle there is nothing wrong with that, but as they were professionals, they should have recognized the 'dangerous' consequences for the company culture and the implications of alienating employees by introducing new HR-related IT systems. In that case they should have acted more carefully and possibly differently, as they had a responsibility for the human capital. That is why they, as HR, exist! It started to make HR vulnerable, as their professional image deteriorated. Intranet systems in companies helped to speed up reporting and (financial) control. Recruitment activities used the Internet or the intranet, and the interviews component of the selection procedures were conducted via Skype.

As the enormous influences of this IT revolution in companies became clear, top managements introduced new IT systems everywhere in their companies. They had to. They created a new corporate IT top position, next to the CEO and the Chief Finance Officer (CFO). This IT and its systems made enormous cost savings like outsourcing possible in the business world. All attention was focused on these newly created phenomena, but IT also had a cost.

Because of these developments a new HR developed, one not based on professional functions but rather on specialist functions like remuneration, pension, or recruitment, all based on IT solutions and connections. Everything was communicated via the computer. It was quick, and it provided an immediate overview and insight. Reporting, questions, performance scores, and bonus calculations—to mention a few business activities—were all handled via the net. The negative development was that verbal discussions between employees and HR staff were limited, sometimes only possible during conferences or via telephone conversations; however, each person had his or her specialism. The answer they were easily giving was *no*—it was not in or according to the 'book'; those were the rules established by the head office. (If the staff member responded in the affirmative then the person had to do something and discuss matters with his or her boss, which could lead to problems and could create exceptions. So it was better to say *no*. Problem solved.)

The employee was put in a box with his or her position score and that gave them their possibilities and limitations. HR became very powerful by introducing this. Even an MD or GM was no longer responsible for the traditional HR positions in his or her company (as HR was normally part of the total company management). HR was seen and used by top management as a way to cut costs and increase contribution to the stakeholders. Board members must have been happy with this development, and finally HR, in their new role as 'business partner', got what they wanted: to contribute to the company result! (Something that historically it had been blamed for not doing.) However, it was at a price. They lost the contact and trust of the employees. Slogans often used during the last century, such as 'Our people are our most important capital' and 'We must nurture our company culture' became hollow phrases, not lived up to any more, which everybody could feel and see. Many companies experienced this, and now they all look the same.

Human resources, from being a service provider, became finally a powerhouse, but it ended as an administrator. It executed and followed the 'book'.

For such a position you do not need a professional HR any more. Anybody can do it: the financial manager or any other manager. You simply act as an administrator. That development will show that it is a costly loss for companies.

Local HR departments were reduced in staff to the extent that they were more or less eliminated, with HR being centralized per country or region or even globally. In spite of that, HR as a 'business partner' became a power in itself: an anonymous, cold department, controlling employees, conditions, benefits, and remuneration. There were no exceptions. There was no concern for the company culture. There was no individual care any more. It caused fear among the employees. It went bankrupt. HR lost the trust of employees, its function as a service partner, its professionalism, its innovation, and its being a binding and responsible factor in representing the human capital in a company.

The circle is complete from administrator to administrator in fifty years.

B. 'YOU GET WHAT YOU WANT TO HEAR'

'You get what you measure' is what top management, your bosses, or head offices want to hear and what they believe it does. I have personally experienced in the last ten years that that is not always the case and that what is reported does not always reflect the reality. The result of this administration mentality, which I described before, is that top management became short-sighted and wanted a quick fix. I became frustrated and disappointed when I got to know and experienced the results of some of the so-called cost-reduction companies, benchmarking left and right and promising a lot of benefits that would result in a better bottom line. Some of them are good, well-thought-through, and proven to work, at least in some companies, but what I could not understand was why these responsible top managers/executives never made use of the potential in their own organization. Mobilize them. Involve their companies and management. Make use of the unique possibilities that a company culture can bring you. No other company can beat that. Have they tried many times and given up? Or does it cost them too much energy to drive it by themselves in their own company? HR, as an innovator, can contribute very much here by making use of the company's own unique human capital factor, but they do not.

On the contrary, in HR circles cost reduction and cutting of HR headcount are the main arguments to make a financial contribution to the bottom line. At the same time a kind of replacement do-it-yourself system is introduced, taking away a lot of HR administration in local companies, bringing down HR staff, and letting employees fill in and communicate—a costly IT program specially developed for HR. It will reduce many local HR positions and give rise to a new concentration of so-called competence centres, in regions or globally, resulting in a uniform, streamlined, and efficient HR! At least that is the way it is sold. Regional specialists, managed by central HR, take over the function of the local HR and that of the local MD/GM and run the 'show'.

I have never experienced such a short-sighted, top-down action with such a disastrous result. Everywhere you hear criticisms, in particular feelings of alienation by employees concerning what is going on. They are scared that they will lose their job, and they are scared about raising objections (as objections are not accepted). In this difficult period economically, people stay in the company, silent, as many told me. So it looks like a successful introduction. 'You want to hear that!' But what you see is demotivation, confusion, and negativism. You hear everywhere, from young and old, that they do not understand it. Talk to employees in a bar, during a sporting activity, at a birthday party, or at a family reunion, and you will hear everywhere identical frustrations—and they won't be people from the same company!

Some companies have realized this mistake and are trying to correct it, but in the meantime it has caused enormous damage to the company culture, the loyalty, and the trust. It created a cynical group of once loyal workers. It will come at a cost. It is not one that can be quantified yet, but it will come.

I have many questions regarding the cost-reduction arguments related to HR. Yes, it was growing too fast in the past, it became bureaucratic, and it probably had too many employees in the period of multi-tasking. If you now notice the high costs of IT to handle HR systems and the 'specialists' allocated in regional centres, then you will come to the conclusion that there must be cheaper ways. For instance, local, 'low'-paid HR employees in an emerging market are dismissed and replaced by new high-paid regional HR staff in an expensive country. Or 'expensive' HR employees are replaced by a low-cost country where HR made a regional set-up but where there are language or cultural difficulties and related communication problems and the number of staff in the location is not much smaller than in the old form. Is that bringing the service closer to the employees? All focus is now on uniformity and the 'book'. Local HR is gone. Probably the new created costs are no longer called HR costs but are shifted to other non-fixed cost centres. The finance people will be happy with this outcome. However, it is wrong, in my opinion, because I doubt if the cost reduction is a valid argument.

Now as the headcount in HR is cut dramatically, the headcount argument, probably as a result of benchmarking with other companies and multinationals, is solved. Is that such an important argument? Only wanting to be in-line with other multinationals? In emerging countries you have more people but often at lower costs. Initially you need a strong HR to introduce the company values and culture. Or is that not the case any more? What is so important about the headcount argument? Efficiency? Yes, that remains a good argument and needs attention. Too many people or a too 'fat' organization, also in HR, is not acceptable and is something that has to be addressed. There are many good ways to handle this. But why kill it?

In my opinion top management has lost the relation and contact with the work floor; they no longer see or hear what is going on. Due to the so-called fast information systems they have little interest in meeting workers/employees; they do not see or experience the enormous potential of a culture of loyalty. It is unpaid loyalty that can be seen in giving extra attention to quality awareness and avoiding claims; in the extra time (often unpaid) that employees give to a company in the case of urgent orders; and in the sales person or service engineer being tired after a lot of trips abroad but again taking the next trip to another customer. There are numerous examples that could be given to illustrate what motivation and loyalty in the right company culture are contributing to a company. The inherent risk is that you do not get 'your' people committed and motivated any more. (Even board members should have contact with employees; they are often selected CEOs of other companies, so they should have an interest.) Figures, figures, and benchmarking are the new reality. They are important, but the solutions are close by and are completely ignored. Try to be inventive and creative and try to do it yourself, using the strength of a company. 'Try to listen to what your people want!' Is that ever tried seriously?

You can always bring in consultants at a later stage, but the solution is in the company! Use it! It will cost extra work and energy, but start with it! It is a risk of course because you and HR have to do it yourselves. Do not outsource. However, consultants are still brought in—possibly because the person who is responsible wants to hide behind them.

For the sake of headcount reduction in HR, the company is 'killed' from the inside.

Companies are flexible, and some of the 'old' roles of the local HR will be taken over by other functions or people. That can be a union leader, a works council, a medical doctor, a lawyer, or even the internal post delivery person, to mention some examples. If informal leaders stand up to take their new roles, professionals or not, they will fill the vacuum of having no local HR. This vacuum is created by a centrally organized HR with no personal care in their program any more! Do not underestimate the strength of a local company! It is all happening beyond the control of the new centralized HR, which is much worse. Their company loyalty is different because they reacted as a result of there being less attention paid to the human capital in the company.

The installed IT systems will remain, but they should be re-evaluated as they are often useless systems that nobody uses in reality. It gives head office control of a lot of personal data and that creates fear. Fear to be controlled. Fear to be dismissed. Result: 'You get what you want to hear.' That's all; nobody will take the input seriously any more, and it does not reflect the reality. The workers and people in the field know how to survive. In many countries they are used to these kinds of requests in other political systems from the past, such as the USSR. From the outside it all looks good, but the reality is completely different. I experienced that myself in a few countries. How can you run a company from a distance with such output?

Top management had 'gold' in their hands with a unique company culture and the loyalty of employees, which could solve a lot of problems, create efficiency, flexibility, and cost savings if properly managed and followed up. That is the gold. It has now been destroyed by almighty benchmarking meetings in Paris, London, or New York to be the best-in-class among colleagues/competitors or due to stock market and/or shareholders' pressure to make the share price go up and to make the score as good as possible. The solution has been neglected, which they had in-house. Is it a case of blindness, arrogance, and having lost contact with the base? They are all question marks, but the 'gold' is gone.

C. ACTUAL OBSERVATIONS IN HUMAN RESOURCES' PRACTICE

There are many companies and many examples that show the actual situation in HR departments. I received many reactions when I explained that I planned to write this booklet concerning the situation in companies related to HR. Not one was positive! Everybody came up with examples of how 'bad' the situation is. They spoke of 'alienation' caused by the IT revolution and by the described actions of HR and the related company, which was once a good employer, according to their workers, and one that they were loyal to in the past. Lack of motivation and a waste of good positive energy was the result. It is an enormous risk for companies to lose its most valuable resource: human capital.

It is not only the difficult economic situation that some companies are in that worries people but that they don't feel supported any more and that they have no trust in HR. They try to handle their requests and discuss problems with their immediate superior or with the MD/CEO directly, often with good results. They experience HR only as an obstacle in their attempts to solve their requests and problems.

It is a pity to write this, as I noticed a complete deterioration of, in principle, a good profession in HR. Especially in this IT time HR has an important new role to play—to re-energize the company and return to their HR roots, instead of being a 'business partner'. Top management must see that it is the wrong development for HR and for the company! I simply do not understand how staff and managers can act towards their employees/colleagues or even to interested applicants in such a way that you get so many negative reactions. Something is completely wrong.

Below are a few examples and some of the arguments of the many I have received, which the reader for sure will recognize.

a. A young undergraduate applied via the Internet on the website of a company, one of the biggest in the UK, for an apprenticeship position, as they were looking for candidates. The person spent the entire Sunday filling in all of the questionnaires. He also had to write an essay about his motivation and why he was interested in working for that company. Finally on the evening of that Sunday he was ready and sent the documentation by email to the company. To his surprise he received an automatic response forty-five minutes later that was a decline of his application, stating that the company was not interested in him. Most likely, the software made a selection on some key answers and based on that, calculated that this person had not enough points to continue. Is this HR? The persons responsible within that company for installing or buying such a system, probably because of efficiency reasons, must have been arrogant and blind to do this. Even if you receive 1,000 or 10,000 applications, you can think of better solutions. With such an experience, do you think this person will ever use the products of this company? And that is not to mention the people he will tell about this experience. How much harm will this do to that company?

b. Another young person was looking for a job. She had a qualified bachelor education and was sending more than 200 mails to existing open vacancies (all around the world) via email. She received only five reactions out of 200, of which two were negative. With three companies she had interviews via Skype, and finally she got a job offer to work in Dubai, which she gladly accepted. A total of 195 companies with vacancies did not reply. Not even a short reply. Is this HR? A typical response from many people would be, 'Oh that is normal; it works like that', but is there not a way as a company that you can profile yourselves in a better way? Do you realize how much harm is done to all these companies who are too arrogant or too lazy to send even a short reply? It also hurts the HR image very much. What will people think of such a department?

c. An incentive like a performance bonus system based on a balanced scorecard is an overdone system and is outdated as an action to motivate people. On the contrary, how often do you hear, 'It's not in my BSC' or 'It's not part of my BSC'. It does not motivate people to do things outside their BSC measurements or to look for other improvements. There are better systems/methods available that are also less costly.

Be creative! Do not always follow what other companies or consultants are trying to sell you!

This BSC and performance system creates greed. In terms of, 'You get what you measure', yes, you get that, but it is very short-sighted and missing at the end the final overall company goal: to create a long-lasting culture that secures the future of the company. BSC was positive as a short-term action, and that is it.

In the meantime it destroys the culture, which took decennia to nurture and build. Is HR supporting this?

d. In difficult economic times short-term results are often needed in order to keep the bottom line healthy or to limit a negative result in order to satisfy the stakeholders.

Lean manufacturing or lean management are just examples, and many more cost-saving systems have been introduced in companies. As management, especially HR, you must be aware of the fact that you are playing with certain 'elasticity' within the workforce. Sometimes it looks like top management is no longer interested in the long term and that they are introducing one cost saving action after the other. But if these actions go on for years while the results of these actions may be positive and the company may be in better shape, there will come a moment when the worker's 'elasticity' will be gone. Then lean management is seen as just another way to squeeze more out of them, and people will become rebellious. Lean will become mean: a mean HR.

I have experienced and discovered myself obstructions that have been carried out on purpose, that is, sabotage. These have been carried out by employees simply because of hatred, a lack of interest in the company, and a loss of interest in their own future. Quality went down, and claims were created on purpose in order to 'hit' the company, which lost customers. These are problems that you can only solve locally, and we managed to do so with success. Central HR or top management will often react in the wrong way and will make the situation only worse, as they do not understand the motives that were historically grown (such as strikes, bad management, and bad payment).

e. Employees can, via the HR web, ask questions, apply for internal promotion, follow their scorecard result and so forth. Often you have to report to HR every six months or once a year about ambitions, education need, and similarly. All is anonymous and rather cold. It creates a distance, and there is no relation with HR any more, as they are often no longer physically present in a company. This will lead to people looking for other alternatives themselves. The Internet gives them a kind of 'freedom', particularly with social media like Facebook and Twitter. HR will have no grip any more on these informal activities.

We had a similar experience with our bank, one of the top five in the world, in Jakarta, Indonesia. Once we settled in, we applied for an account and were welcomed very nicely. We were even introduced to our account manager.

Two years later, the bank re-organized, and all account managers disappeared because of cost reasons. The bank became smaller, and we only could communicate via an open television monitor in a big room, where everybody could listen to and see us. A person appeared on the screen, and with him or her you had to talk about financial problems, overdrafts, investments and so on. Privacy was completely gone. Is this the new way you handle your customers? We left that bank and found a very good and service-minded local bank. Is that what we can also expect dealing with HR? People will leave or look for alternatives?

f. A young person finalized his study with good results and started his first job in an international company. His salary was basic, but he accepted it because he liked the job, and it was a difficult time to find a job. After one year of work to the satisfaction of his employer, he was offered a permanent position. He noticed that his former study colleagues were earning in the region of about 30% to even 50% more than him. He asked HR what his future was and what his salary prospect was by the end of the year. He was hoping for a raise, to come in line with his working colleagues and his market value. He was expecting a raise of 30% to 40%, possibly done in two steps.

The HR person told him that he could count, as everybody else in their labour agreement, on an increase of 1.5%!

A 1.5% raise could be an increase for a person on his maximum salary level, but for a young graduate you should have attention for his or her situation and salary level if you want to keep him or her. An evaluation once or twice a year is needed to bring him or her in line and get the best out of him or her. Is this HR? What do you think that person will do? For sure he will not discuss his case with HR any more but look for another solution that suits him.

g. 'This is the biggest reason talented young employees quit their job' is the title of a blog by Annie Murphy Paul (*The Brilliant Blog*, 18 September 2012). It is also a study in *Harvard Business Review*, published in the summer of 2012, that confirmed that young employees are leaving in droves. The reasons: there is no attention paid to their training/ education; there is no career development; and there are no salary adjustments for young starters. 'Respect and fairness is not on the work floor anymore', 'Companies have no loyalty to their workers' and 'I just skip for better opportunities' were some of the comments. Because of the economic crisis, companies pay low and play low, but young graduates do not accept that. Young people want a personal and clearly articulated career path. Mentoring and coaching is what is asked for. Where is HR?

The above examples confirm it: HR is sick; it is bankrupt; and it has lost its professional attitude. (It is not service minded any more and has lost respect from employees.)

SECTION 2

How HR can regain trust and respect and fulfil the right role in a company management team

D. GENERAL MANAGEMENT AND HUMAN RESOURCES: LESSONS TO BE LEARNED

Based on my eighteen years of working in general management I have a lot to share about my experiences in this important position, as a GM or an MD of a company, in different countries. The GM position and HR are linked, and the GM can be of great help to give HR the right role in his or her management team, so it can regain the trust and respect it has lost. It will help the overall functioning of the company! That is why I describe separately the MD/GM and HR priorities of how I see their tasks. The main objective of HR must be that all parties in a company must be united for the same goal: to make the company better and profitable. For instance, they could be united in the development of new products or production methods, with the aim to secure the future of a company for all their stakeholders. Here HR can contribute by selecting the right people, suggesting a new organization, and suggesting new ideas as to how people and management can work together. We must be willing to change, especially in difficult circumstances, such as loss of market share, quality problems, wrong products, lack of sales channels, strong competition, or poorly functioning internal organization. It all reflects a difficult (financial) situation for a company.

1. The local unique company

As often is said, but not often accepted and understood by head offices, each country is unique. There are big differences between the Nordic countries and the Baltics and between Belgium and The Netherlands. Each company also (even those situated in the same country), new or established, big or small, with a simple or complicated organizational structure, is unique. If you can accept this as a base, your decisions can be very successful, as you will have the local and typical culture as your starting point. Here a local HR can play a role to advise company management.

Each company is based on its history, products, ownership, and origin. On top of which, it is dynamic. It changes due to developments in markets, changes in local laws, and as a consequence of social and political changes.

New ideas like quality circles, management development, lean manufacturing, and world class manufacturing are adopted by big and small companies. What is a success in one country/company is not automatically a success in another company/country or even in a multinational! It needs the involvement of top management, and it has to be studied, implemented, and adjusted to the situation(s) of the specific company/country. This is often overlooked or ignored, with disastrous results. HR has an important role to play here!

Nowadays it looks like top management and board members act like sheep: They blindly follow new ideas from well-known consultants, gurus, or institutes with famous names, instead of nurturing and learning from their own company's uniqueness, successes, failures, and culture! The success of a 'new' idea is often dubious or short lived—existing until the next new 'idea' comes up.

Often companies and countries are organized in groups, clusters, regions, and divisions and are managed together under the mottos of control and efficiency according to similarity in products, (multinational) customer base, channel to the market and so forth. The same arguments are used to bring HR departments together in one central HR per country, a region, or even centrally covering the globe. We have to ask: Do these decisions harm the market position and business climate of the company or not? Do they cause a loss in market share? Do they really bring the planned cost savings? Has anybody checked it? Has anybody provided feedback, so we can learn from a success or failure?

2. Managing director/General manager

As MD/GM you should pay attention to the following:

*The start. You have arrived in this company (and often new country, with your family), briefed by your bosses in head office, including why they sent you and, in particular, what the problems are (in their eyes), probably mostly related to finance, quality, and organization.

*Your management team, representing the important functions/ departments in the company like sales, finance, production, engineering, after-sales services, supply chain, HR, IT, quality control (QC), and product groups.

*Getting the priorities right from the beginning. If you have to manage a company, whether small or big, with only sales activities or one completely integrated with sales, engineering, and production you need to consider what is the task. Is it growth? Is it to develop new sales channels? Is it to develop new products? Is it to re-organize or re-engineer the company?

*Developing and coaching a strong management team.

*Taking responsibility for your employees and their families. All eyes of the workers are on you! If you calculate the number of employees and multiply it by four (to take account of partners and children) then you will have an idea of the responsibility you have, especially when a company is in trouble.

*The two important common underlying fundaments that affect everybody in a company: finance (without finance it does not work) and HR (without good and trained people you are nowhere). It covers all departments! These two fundaments will decide if a company will become a success or failure. They also affect the respective leaders/managers.

*Being the coordinator of all the contacts that your different departments have with related (regional and global) supporting structures in departments like supply chain, sales, and production.

*Setting targets and creating a new enthusiasm with achievable goals for the company, your management team, and all employees. Communications is the key to getting the new objectives and priorities understood and accepted. Some companies prepare a 'slogan' to motivate everybody around the new goals like 'Yes, we can' or 'We try harder'. But a slogan alone does not work.

*Setting the example *all* of the time. If you do this then people will start to believe you, and you will get them slowly on your side. For instance, providing goals and initiatives to stop the high number of claims has to be followed up by focusing on motivation, the involvement of all employees and the workers' council, quality awareness actions, training, and possibly a new remuneration system. Other goals can include increase in sales and the development of new markets.

Whatever actions and initiatives you prepare for, it must be clear that you will have to choose. Only one or two main goals are necessary to get your people around the actions that you and your team are starting to prepare. If you feel that you are not getting your plans accepted, stop it and investigate what went wrong before making a new start. HR has a very important role to play in all these preparations and even more so in the next chapter. When the goals are set and accepted, the execution phase asks for a different action from you.

*The *service function* to support the development of the different departments in the execution of the set goals. It is needed to give direction, sometimes to correct, but most of the time to suggest new ideas and new ways and open doors to new contacts. I had once a boss/superior who called me at the weekend with the opening question, 'Hi, Rudolf, what can I do for you?' He was serious and also supported and helped when needed. I must admit that with all the many other bosses I had had, this had never happened to me before. But it is the right attitude. Support your people. Give service. Then you get enthusiasm, commitment, and a team focused on the set objectives: We have to solve a bad situation and turn it around. The decisions, what to do and execute, are based on the local circumstances, finances, and people; it also limits, at least in time, your 'own big plans', that is, what you had in mind when you accepted the job.

* The support from the HR manager/director and the department. If you will be responsible for a 'turn around' of a company, which is a difficult and time-consuming process, you will need all the support from the HR manager/director and the department. Both the GM

and the HR have to investigate the situation in the company in that particular country. Each company and each country is, as earlier stated, unique.

*The introduction of global or regional decisions. When these decisions are introduced you and your management team have to evaluate how to introduce them and where problems could arise because of the unique local situation. This is to avoid misunderstandings and failures. All these global initiatives have to be translated to the local situation. Most of these initiatives can be implemented without a problem, as they are logical and general, but not all, and each of them has to be discussed and checked first, especially with regard to how to inform the organization about it.

Sometimes a global initiative has to be postponed because of internal (local) developments or possibly because the local MD is the obstacle (right or wrong, but it has to be investigated). Each company has developed a culture during decennia of operation. Not all company cultures are positive.

*Distrust. Because of many takeovers, strikes, low salaries, discrepancies between management and workers, and frequent changes of MD, distrust has developed. Suspicion arises towards the ideas of this new 'arrogant MD with his big new car and big house'. Informal leaders and union activities in the company can be a challenge to overcome. It will be difficult to erase suspicion and regain trust. But it can be done together with your local HR department, and I always experienced this as the biggest challenge! That is why you took this job and why they selected you to do this job! Now you can show your competence as leader and coach.

- It is also important to watch the environment of your company.
- Is it in an emerging market, a booming economy or not?
- Social welfare systems: Are they existing or not?
- Neighbour relations: Are they friendly towards the company or not (noise problems)?
- Local laws can limit your plans.
- Religious tensions: Are they existing in a company/country or not?

A long list of checkpoints and selected objectives will help you to prepare a realistic roadmap of actions and priorities to start with.

As MD I worked 60% on organizational/HR items and 40% on the rest, mainly on finance issues, sales negotiations, customer visits, and production matters (often linked to HR). It became clear to me and more and more obvious that a local problem needs a local solution. Of course that is not to say that expertise and advice can be given by a central HR service, if there is competence and an interest to do so, with the goal to help you, not to create more obstacles. Otherwise you and your team will have to do it yourself.

3. Human resources

The MD, as the end decision maker, and HR can make a great contribution to the company culture in a country, which motivates people. The HR manager/director and his or her staff must act as a service provider and must be able to understand the value and importance of a company culture. A company culture is recognized and sometimes written down *after* a company has been developing for many years. Covering both good and bad times, it is the sum of unwritten feelings, of relations, and the inner workings of a company and its workers. It is shown in all activities, and the outside world can notice this. It is unique and, often the company and their workers are proud of this. The people in that company have made that culture, based on their history, and they have continued to develop it. It often has 'hidden' rules, traditions, and expectations. But it is not static. It changes.

HR, working properly, should be the 'godfather' of this culture and the specialist of the local culture in the company/country. Next to that, they have the competence in the ABC (recruitment, selection, training and so on) of HR, conflict and problem solving, career development, employee relations, labour (union) contacts, and contracts and knowledge related to occupational health problems, loans, retired employees' items, social and medical cases. All of these HR activities have an influence towards a company culture, which determines for a great part the success of a company, and it is impossible to copy them for use in other companies. A lot of companies follow like sheep new slogans or developments (that is, new corporate 'fashions' as I call them), suggested by well-known international consultant companies or company gurus. They incorporate them into their own organization without realizing their own particular situation and culture, with often a failure as a result. Of course expertise and competence from the outside can be useful, effective, and a learning curve for a company. Not all is 'bad', but we should not act like sheep, and we need to be critical as to how and when we use outside expertise.

Even since the Industrial Revolution (I mention at random, Keynes, Ford, and the early textile industry), organizational problems have continued to exist, and the same problems have occurred as in the 'old' days. They are not new, but all the time we put a new name on a 'new' solution for these problems. Some have been useful like quality system programs based on Japanese experiences. But it often did not last long. Why not? Because it was not invented here? Or was it because it was not part of our own culture?

My experience is that we should use our own competences and creativity to solve these problems! The people make the company! It is the 'culture' that decides the success or failure of a new organizational set-up or a new directive from head office. That is why local HR and local management are so interlinked and important in the execution of new directives or changes of whatever kind. They know how to implement them, in what time frame and how to translate them into local actions. By doing this, such a 'new' HR will be respected and trusted. It will give the function the correct role in a management team. I have experienced successes with this way of working in Spain, The Netherlands, Russia, and Indonesia.

I have managed a number of big re-organizations like for example in The Netherlands and Russia, including a lot of redundancies, by using the competence from local HR and a good planning to successfully execute this without 'big' problems. I managed to still maintain the respect of the workforce because everybody understood that it was necessary. Sometimes we were assisted by local HR specialists outside the company in that country, especially for legal advice.

4. HR has a public relations task

Although HR and the MDs who work with them have specific functions, perhaps one of the most important functions is the public relations (PR) task. It is not often recognized and it is often neglected by top management and even HR professionals. But the HR department is the company's human face for the workers and the public relations, good and bad, can have a big impact on the company's culture and its future.

As HR, they, on many occasions, represent the company, also when the head office is based far away. All activities that they undertake as well as the ways in which they do them are the subjects of discussions by workers at home, in the company, between family and friends, and even government officials when they visit the company. The way they recruit, select, handle re-organizations, dismissals, medical problems, company accidents, and the salaries, are just a few of the examples. The company is monitored, and whether the company is doing things in the wrong or right ways, it all reflects on the image of the company in that country: positive or negative. In my opinion, all these activities by the company and representation by HR must have a fundament of care and fairness. That makes a company image strong, solid, and honest. Government representatives when visiting the company want to see you as an example for other companies.

- Organize neighbour days.
- Provide an open house for workers and their families.
- Family gatherings are just a few activities that have a PR function too.

- Visit sick workers or be supportive when extra medical help is needed.
- Be concerned as to our security and how we care about the security of our workers.
- Attend the funerals of deceased employees.

Show sympathy and involvement as a company; it is all part of the company culture. You can feel with such a culture that you can manage the problems the company is facing. It shows commitment, stability, and success. It will also help you to attract good, motivated applicants who want to work in such a company!

The culture decides the success or failure of a new organizational set-up or directive. Head office is often not aware of the enormous impact the activities of a local HR has in a country for the company! It increases innovation, creates success, and supports the bottom line of a company—that I can guarantee!

E. Fun in and at work

1. Fun in work

In a time of economic crisis and all kinds of doom scenarios, although still quite a lot of countries/companies do well, it is more important than ever to keep your workers motivated. Obstruction and even the word 'sabotage' are not on their minds. On the contrary! They enjoy their work and have pleasure, most of the time, at work. It delivers quality! It leads to work well done and satisfaction. Below are some positive examples of a new HR, one that contributes in creating a 'winning team'.

*Selection is the right and only good instrument to attract the right people for an open position. HR is involved, knowing the culture and the department structure where the vacancy exists. And together with the manager they know who to select to make a change in a department or for other reasons to establish continuation. Try to avoid outsourcing this! Do it yourself and then you will have control of who is joining the company. Central HR can be of help supplying expertise in selection or selection methods. Involve future colleagues as speaking partners with applicants. Not only should the company select but also the candidate! This is to avoid misunderstandings and too high expectations. If you follow this procedure, I can guarantee you that most of the newly employed people will be happy and will do a good job in the company.

*HR and the manager of the new employees must follow and stimulate new recruits. Keep an eye on their market value and have a good and fair remuneration system (providing a twice-a-year evaluation for new employees in the first two years). For the longer employed, persons must be kept alert, and if they want to change position or have an increase in salary, discussions should take place about the possibilities related to their competence and capacities.

*Do not promise openings or positions you cannot deliver, especially when employees do not have the capacity for it. Too often managers are weak or soft when it comes to handling these difficult situations, and local HR can be of assistance in making sure that it is handled professionally. Be fair. Do not play politics in these sensitive matters, as employees feel that immediately.

*Job rotation, project work, or rotating colleagues between different departments helps to create 'fun' in work, which means enthusiasm, loyalty towards colleagues and the company, helping one another in cases of problems and not following and creating a 'blame' culture. It takes time and energy to make this happen, but the rewards are very encouraging.

The company is always changing; it is always moving to be ahead of the competition, ready to launch new products, new production techniques, or new engineering solutions. The workers are part of that process. It is impossible to create 100% job satisfaction, but HR and the supervisors/managers have a task here to follow the motivation of their employees. As MD you must drive, initiate, and support these changing new activities in order to keep the company moving.

*Appraisal/Performance systems when done correctly twice or at least once a year will give a lot of information to the manager about the situation and the 'temperature'(atmosphere) in his or her department. Follow-up of the promises or suggestions made by the manager is crucial if such a system will work. Frequent discussions will avoid misunderstanding and de-motivation. Employees need challenges but also rewards.

*Treat people in the same way that you want to be treated by your superior(s), which they unfortunately may not often do. If that is the case, according to your opinion, then that is even more reason to handle your own people the correct way.

The mentioned HR activities like selection, pay, job mobility, and care are related to employee relations; they create 'fun' in work, and that needs constant attention. The created atmosphere and culture in a company must give the employees the possibility to develop themselves, even in simple routine jobs. Allow them to make mistakes, and correct them if necessary. Support them, and with the right management to coach them, 'fun' and enthusiasm are created in the workplace, in a place of administration, in an engineering office, or in a factory. As a result, there will be success in the company, and visitors will make compliments about the quality or the way that the company is organized. That is the best motivator, better even than a bonus. People like to get compliments. When these kinds of successes are created, like getting orders in, everybody is involved in and proud of this result. You can see how proud they are on their faces! Then you have created a winning team. Experienced auditors from suppliers and other companies can often 'feel' immediately if the atmosphere in a company is the right one. You can check that, they will tell you.

It is the best sales tool to be used, to get more and new orders in, as they provide the customer with a sense of trust and quality that this company is well managed. It is proven in different assignments, and customers told me themselves when they placed a new order!

2. Fun at work

Management must have an eye for this and take initiatives to create the right atmosphere. For instance, if a big project has been delivered and a lot of overtime has been clocked over a short period of time, you have to do something to release the stress and to thank the employees and compliment them. However, as an MD/GM first you must know what kind of sacrifices your employees made to get an order in or a delivery on time! Unfortunately some MDs do not even know what is happening in their own company!

Below are positive examples of an involved HR working closely with the GM! These are actions that support the atmosphere, for example to celebrate the closure of a big project or another important event.

- Take the group out! Have a nice dinner as a thank you for the extra work done. Involve yourself in the sacrifices that your people have made. Let the workers decide what they want to do to celebrate. Cultivate a success. Take pictures.

- Sending a bouquet of flowers or sending a cake to the partner of the employee is not a bad idea.

- A management team working under stress needs attention. Initiate a relaxing Friday afternoon meeting, with some drinks and food, as we did in Indonesia. There should be no agenda; the idea should simply be to relax and exchange what happened during the last week. People go home with a better feeling. In some countries (Spain, Sweden, The Netherlands, and Russia) we went to a bar or had some fun in the canteen. It was simply to relax and to come closer to one another and sometimes to correct a mistake or to come to terms with an angry colleague.

- HR has an important role to play here as an organizer and/or initiator and in order to control the process. It is not the costs that count; what you get back from the togetherness, fun, and belonging as part of a great team is enormous and not to be quantified.

- In some countries, Christmas parties or breaking-the-fast in Muslim countries are traditions; all such traditions create a good atmosphere and a feeling of working for a good company.

- As stated earlier, enjoy 'open house' initiatives for families of employees. Family gatherings, sporting activities, neighbour days (that is, inviting the neighbours around your premises) all help to create a relaxing and informal gathering outside working hours. They create unity. Human Resources, again, are crucial in these activities and, at the same time, it involves the workers and their representatives. It clears the way for a new week or new day at work. Fun at work. 'Fun' does not have to be expensive and pays dividends into the company culture, which in turn helps everyone.

F. A REVIVAL AND RECOGNITION OF HR: REGAINING TRUST AND RESPECT

This section is concerned with suggestions and recommendations for a properly functioning HR.

In this booklet I concentrated on HR, my vision based on my experiences. Of course as MD/GM of a company you have more than the HR department to manage, but the GM and HR are very closely related to prepare the right conditions for a company to develop and to grow. Other departments as part of your general manager's task will not be discussed in this book but in my next book about 'general management'.

Below are crucial suggestions for implementation to repair the lack of trust and respect in HR.

1. I have written about the importance of HR for the whole company and especially about the importance of a local HR in a company in a country. As an example, I have talked

about their role in supporting the business, as public relations officers, and their contribution to a local company culture (which can be used as a sales tool). Local HR can work as the link between a central head office-related HR policy and a local company to translate and embed that policy into a local structure. It is a fact that local circumstances decide the success or failure of a centrally or globally issued directive or advice. So a local HR is needed to deal with the ABC of HR and all employee relation issues. Of course global or central support and expertise is welcome, needed, and appreciated, and guidelines are necessary to create a global HR policy, but the unique local situation must be understood, recognized, and honoured in this policy. *Instead of 'one solution fits all', you get a corporate policy as a kind of quilt, a patchwork* of different colours, representing the unique circumstances in each company and country. It will make the whole company more successful, vibrant, and multicultural, thanks to this new HR policy.

2. Continue to focus on the *improvement of the competences* of the employees (training and education).

3. Future *MD candidates should be selected on their HR competence* and interest. They should not be selected only on their sales or engineering background.

4. Constantly try to work to create an efficient organization. If cost reductions are necessary and are centrally suggested or demanded, let the *local MD and his or her staff in the country decide* about the best way to realize such a cost

reduction, eventually involving all departments and workers. Let top management show the trust in the local MD and the local HR by allowing them to do it. I myself have done that successfully in several international assignments. The MD needs to have intuition as to where, when, and how to start such a program.

5. Make *use of IT systems* that can speed up the information flow but only if proven useful. Sometimes a lot of data are collected without any purpose or use. Critical follow-up is needed, as IT costs are extremely high. This group and their costs are growing fast in many companies, and there is a lack of cost control in their activities.

6. Recruitment of professionally educated HR staff will help to develop the HR department into a service provider for all employees. Specialists like lawyers, psychologists, and other experienced persons in management are welcome too, as long as the attitude of the selected person is *service minded*. A mix of different managerial and educational backgrounds in a HR team with the right leadership can work very positively and create innovative ideas. That is what we expect from HR!

7. HR exists because you have to deal with exceptions. If you do not accept or tolerate exceptions, then you do not need an HR. You just follow the 'book', and the answer to a request is often *no*, as no exceptions are tolerated. That is the direction in which it developed and one of the reasons for me writing this book. We work with human beings, and as a result

unique solutions are sometimes needed. *Exceptions* must be handled openly and fairly so that we can stand up in front of all employees and explain why we have acted in this case as we did. Exceptions do not need to cost money, but it can be to give extra attention to an employee with a family tragedy or the organization of a second opinion in case of a medical check as needed in some countries. With the exceptions you show the real company's intention of a good, well-balanced HR policy, which contributes to its specific culture. You do not need to be a soft HR person, but you do need to be a fair one, which can be very tough too!

8. The MD, as the end decision maker, and HR can make a great contribution to the company culture in a country, which motivates people. The combination of and cooperation between the MD and HR as described in this book brings together a unity in company policies towards our human capital. *Care, and be fair.* As we live now in an IT and Internet time, you have to and can do everything yourself. Yes, a lot of people can do, but we need to have a responsibility for *all* employees, also those who cannot or are not able and need assistance. Also IT specialists need attention and care. In this 21st century there are many 'isolated' persons; you find them in engineering, administration, sales, QC, production, and after sales. Even more attention is needed in this time we live in! A good functioning local HR must be present in a company!

SUMMARY

Good, vital companies, each with their own unique culture and way of working, landed in the hands of top management and became the subject of boardroom meetings, where what was discussed looked like normal practice and an excellent visionary approach but where the crucial mistake was made to ignore the unique competences and vitality they had in their hands to solve problems. They let it slip. They were constantly bombarded with figures as a result of IT programs by finance as well as benchmarking, consultants, stakeholders, shareholder pressure, stock exchange movements, and wanting to be 'the best in class'. Too much information can create 'mental jams' where people are only focused on the financial health and short-term perspective of the company and maybe also their bonuses. Greed entered, as, for example, what happened in the banking sector and nearly destroyed it.

Some companies were purchased by (capital) investment companies who cherry-picked what was interesting for them. They closed or sold out the rest. All of these activities were aimed at making money. They would buy a company and after a few years of investments and re-organizations, sell it again. In principle there is nothing wrong with this, but, as was often mentioned in the newspapers and television reports, when another financial scandal appeared, greed was often the reason. A company has to make money and has to be profitable, but there are different ways that can be employed to make this happen. Some of these ways of creating profit are very short-sighted and lead to even more problems and a loss of productivity and profitability down the road. A good human being is critical to both profit and success, and ignoring that, results in a robotic HR that replaces the unique culture, making a company strong. As a result, people look for alternatives. Turnover is high. An informal and fractured culture develops where people support one another and create whatever is acceptable for them.

There are alternatives! I have experienced and executed in difficult circumstances re-engineering (turnaround) operations, mass dismissals, and re-organizations to bring companies back to life. Fortunately, top management did not support selling or closing the company and gave it the chance to be re-organized. By recognizing the culture as a base of action, it has an enormous power and potential to be used. You can bring a new *élan* into the company, a new horizon with a future, if all work together and work hard to get it done. When we executed it, dismissed workers came to me to say thank you. It was not that they were happy, but they were thanking me because of the way we did it. They all understood the need and urgency to act, to save a place for the remaining group. It was handled with care and in a way that was open and fair.

I am neither a Saint nor a guru; I've had my successes and I've had my mistakes. However, the focus of a lot of head offices only on financially oriented discussions and presentations, neglecting their responsibility for their own employees, and neglecting the important role that a (local) HR can play in a company, made me angry and disappointed. This book is the result. The solution of problems is in your own hands, in your own company!

'Care and be fair.'

For the persons who read this book and completely disagree with it, I have a suggestion for you, a 'new' development that can be the next fashionable trend to follow, discuss, and meet about in boardrooms and with top management. Just recently, JAL (Japanese Airlines) went out of bankruptcy and back to the stock exchange. A new set-up was accepted, and the reduced number of employees accepted less pay and less pension rights (in a Japanese society!) plus other conditions in order to get this airline started again. This is not negatively mentioned. These were the actions taken by this company, in these circumstances, in order to bring new life into a company and to make a new start—a new and probably good business case to start with. But to copy it and make it a fashionable trend will go too far for me. For sure, consultancy companies are studying this case already. So you can go to the next meeting/discussion.

Rudolf Hartong

ABOUT THE AUTHOR

Rudolf Hartong, born in 1947, was educated in human resources and worked in The Netherlands as an HR professional until 1988. After that, for the following twenty-four years, he and his family (five children) lived in seven countries, where they encountered and experienced different cultures, religions, and situations which changed their lives.

Retired in 2012, after forty years, of which twenty-two were in human resources and eighteen were in general management, he observed some fundamental changes in human resources that made him worried about the development of this profession. He can call himself an expert in this field and has proven so during his assignments.

He and his wife now live in Switzerland.
For comments and remarks:
rudolfhartong@yahoo.com